Performing Character

PERFORMING CHARACTER

From Stage to Page

WAKE FOREST UNIVERSITY

LIBRARY PARTNERS PRESS
WINSTON SALEM, NORTH CAROLINA

Performing Character by Wake Forest University is licensed under a Creative Commons Attribution 4.0 International License, except where otherwise noted.

ISBN 978-1-61846-130-8

Copyright © 2022 by the Authors

Produced and Distributed By:

Library Partners Press, an imprint of Wake Forest University

1834 Wake Forest Road

Winston-Salem, North Carolina 27106

www.librarypartnerspress.com

Manufactured in the United States of America

Contents

Foreword ix
Introduction xiii
About xix

Main Body

Realizing Home 1

Work in Progress 7

Breathborn(e) 15

A Love Letter to Theatre 21

Audition Day 27

Music and Intention 31

A Hopeful Confidence 37

Lens of Admiration 43

The Hardest Performance 49

After Eden 55

So the Stones Cry Out 71

Acknowledgments 77

FOREWORD

CHRISTINA SORIANO

I recently read about the work of Brazilian-born dancer Mickaella Dantas in a May 2021 *Dance Magazine* edition. Since the age of 12, Dantas has worn a prosthetic leg. The limitless possibilities she explores, particularly within the theme of paradox, intrigued me as a choreographer and dance educator. Dantas described working with Portuguese choreographer Clara Andermatt on a project in 2012 and Andermatt's choreographic prompt to "explore walking backwards as though you are walking forward" as a pivotal moment. Dantas reacted by wearing her prosthetic backwards as she moved in space. This inconceivable image of a dancer arriving and departing at the same time immediately felt like an overarching theme to introduce this powerful collection of essays by Wake Forest University student-artists.

As students were writing these essays, the Covid pandemic forced them and artists everywhere to reimagine how we shared our work, how we continued to stretch and learn, and how we maintained our identities and sense of purpose at a time when we could not gather together in person. Artists always line up on a precipice of uncertainty, with their bodies, hearts, and minds exposed. For our students who contributed to this collection, when uncertainty was paramount in the pandemic, they lined up with ingenuity and a willingness to admit that operating in the unknown can be a source of wisdom. To me, this is what leadership looks like.

When Dantas referenced the work of British anthropologist Tim Ingold who said "every movement I make is also a movement of my attention," a eureka moment of dotted lines connected me from Dantas' article to the wisdom shared in the poignant essays and poems in this collection. I am reminded of Mary Costanza's persistent and painstaking devotion to detail and perfection as a ballet dancer, of Liat Klopouh's powerful resilience gleaned from years of piano training, and Adarian Sneed's heartfelt love letter to her beloved partner: the theatre. I am grateful to Grace Powell for sharing her mature realization that one's perspective can (quietly) be shouted from behind a camera lens and to Brianna Coppolino for her daring and beautiful defiance of singing duets during the Covid pandemic with a friend...safely outdoors for one another and for the forest to hear.

I am overwhelmed by these young artists and scholars' abilities to be brave and vulnerable at the same time. I am grateful they found strength in recognizing that their identities as artists—hyphenated and with the many other complex, interdisciplinary foci in which they devote themselves—give them strength and purpose. They are tremendous Wake Forest ambassadors, and I am grateful for the superpowers they share with us in their artistic work and in their creative, thoughtful writing. May they go on and sparkle in the spaces between agony and ecstasy, awe and wonder, and may they always know their Wake Forest Arts family is deeply proud of them.

As we return to crowded theatres, art galleries, dance studios, music halls, and practice rooms once again, let us remember how the arts and artists carried us through a dark time, and as we reconvene into what Émile Durkheim calls "collective effervescence" once again—may the shared purpose of catharsis: of laughing, crying, learning, and growing together be among the most important things we celebrate. Artists teach us this and demonstrate it over and over again.

These students remind us that this is among our most important experiences as human beings.

Christina Soriano, Associate Provost for the Arts and Interdisciplinary Initiatives, July 15, 2021

INTRODUCTION

ANN PHELPS

...have patience with everything unresolved in your heart and to try to love the questions themselves as if they were locked rooms or books written in a very foreign language. Don't search for the answers, which could not be given to you now, because you would not be able to live them. And the point is, to live everything. Live the questions now. Perhaps then, someday far in the future, you will gradually, without even noticing it, live your way into the answer. Perhaps you do carry within you the possibility of creating and forming, as an especially blessed and pure way of living...

–Rainer Maria Rilke, *Letters to a Young Poet*, #4, translated by Stephen Mitchell

---

In the spring of 2020, I found this familiar and beloved passage from Rilke's letters to the aspiring poet, named as "Mr. Kappus," surfacing in my mind again and again. Each day, students wrote emails, text messages, and set up calls full of questions, uncertainty, and confusion in the early days of social distancing and what we now know would be a years-long pandemic. Students who had found their meaning, identity, and even purpose in how they served their community suddenly found themselves alone and isolated. I had no answers. None of us did. All I could do was invite them to join me as we "lived the questions."

In particular, a few students with backgrounds in dance came to me with a mountain of time on their hands, most of whom had danced for 20-40 hours per week since before they had aged into the double digits. What would they do with the empty hours, lack of discipline, and vacant spaces that had once held such beauty? I felt these questions resonate with me as a musician who suddenly could only sing solos in my kitchen, unsure of whether my voice meant anything if it had been reduced to the proverbial tree falling in the forest with no one around to hear it.

Together, we decided we would fill this time by stepping back from center stage and into a space where we might examine our lives and identities as performers from a distance. Who were we now, as dancers, musicians, actors, and artists? We invited one another to submit creative essays that explored these questions and shared them with one another in a small group reading. And in that space, we encountered the beauty and challenge we had been missing, albeit in a very different form. We began to call our group "Center Page: Performance and Character in Isolating Times." The catharsis and encouragement was healing, and we were immediately inspired to broaden our prompts and invite other Wake Forest students to join our writing circles.

We circulated the following questions to students in theatre, dance, music, and the visual arts, seeking to offer them a new stage during this season of solitude when we might consider how all of our years of inspiration, auditions, rehearsal, and performance had shaped our character. And if you feel so moved, we invite you to consider these same questions even now in your own life—performer or not—as they have proven to evoke new insights time and again for those of us who have been sitting with them for a year:

- Describe a particular day of auditioning or rehearsing. How do you prepare? Where do you go? Who is with

you? What are you seeing, hearing, feeling? What are the greatest challenges you face? What brings you a sense of triumph?
- In order to be doing this work, there are other things you have chosen not to do. What sacrifices have you made to get here? What led you to choose this? What obstacles or voices made it difficult to pursue? Was it worth it then? Is it now? How does this choice impact who you are today?
- What is your ultimate goal or purpose when you perform? What calls you to the stage, studio, or microphone again and again? And if your aspirations are dashed (perhaps by a pandemic or any number of setbacks), what is the meaning of the process you have engaged? How has it contributed to or detracted from your flourishing or that of others?

The response was both broad and deep. Students all over campus found themselves reflecting not only on their lives in the arts, but on their pursuits as scholars, caregivers, and leaders with whom these questions resonated. And while many submitted essays and found deep meaning in that, a core group of brilliant women wanted to offer more to each other and go deeper still.

Ten women committed to gathering online to engage in the practice of creative writing and clarifying their voices with the guidance of memoirist and harpist, Dr. April Stace (*White Knuckle Love*, 2020). With April's support and intentionality, these student writers were able to rely on their substantial academic writing skills and expand them to use language in a new way that allowed for the expression and beauty they were missing in a season of social distancing. Through these writing circles, I witnessed new friendships emerge and deepen and heard new voices break through the noise of expectations and assumptions. Bolstered by their courage and community, I even found myself trying new forms of art and creativity, joining in the writing process alongside them.

As a musician, I have always preferred gigs that were not solitary but helped others find their voices too. I have regularly turned down concerts in pursuit of communal song or given up solos in favor of harmonies. Beautifully, in my work here at Wake Forest as the Director of Programming for the Program for Leadership and Character, I get to conduct qualitative research on how creativity and performance shape character and develop leadership skills while also helping students in the arts and beyond both lead and follow, speak and listen. I have seen defeated juniors shake off burdens and heal from wounds that allowed them to take on new identities and interests. I have sat with tearful first-years who weren't sure they could ever belong here and then watched them grow into powerhouses of campus policy-making and student leadership. I have observed self-described "dilettantes" design new courses of study with their professors and students from small mountaintop towns become leaders of movements. I hear story after story of "imposter syndrome" from students who exude eloquence and poise and grow into public figures in our community. And it is my job to behold it all, which honestly, was starting to feel a bit selfish.

So we decided to take some of these stories and share them with the community in this publication, where others might have the chance to encounter the inspiration that sustains me daily as we all press on in a new world that is still in the throes of a pandemic. I am so excited to share this tiny sliver of the beauty I encounter in these students' lives, though I wish you could have accompanied me in the numerous one-on-one editing sessions we had on the balconies of local coffee shops or the patio of the Leadership and Character offices in Starling Hall or the tiny Zoom rooms where we somehow found wells of communal meaning-making through masks or screens or whatever other barriers existed.

In these essays, we discover that auditions have been places where we can recognize our own power and competence (and sometimes lack thereof) while examining our own biases and tendencies. We see that rehearsals have been spaces where we habituate the capacities that become our default behaviors of resilience or empathy or courage that we integrate into our identities even after the curtain closes. We have learned humility through reflection on our mistakes and confidence through our encounters with beauty. And in the day-to-day of it all, we meet the people who become our castmates, bandmates, company, and friends who will hold us accountable and offer aid when things do not go as planned, when we need to improvise together because the world has shut down and we are all left "yes-anding" each other in hopes we can somehow keep this scene going another day.

It is in this community that we overcome our isolation and find the strength to "live the questions," even when the script is thrown out and we are left making it up as we go. In fact, that moment of uncertainty is where the character of creativity comes alive.

Ann Phelps, Director of Programming for the Program for Leadership and Character, August 2021

ABOUT

"Realizing Home" by Katherine Finch, '22, dancer

> From her perch on the balcony of a renowned ballet school, Katherine wonders what a "normal" life of a teenager might be, only to discover a new world in college where her identity as a dancer and pursuits as a scholar come together to make her feel whole.

"Work in Progress" by Leanna Bernish, '24, painter

> With stunning authenticity, Leanna struggles with how to be a girl, what femininity is, and how scary acrylic paint is until she paints her way into her identity on the canvas and in her own body.

"Breathborn(e)" by Brianna Coppolino, '22, singer

> In this breathtaking poem, the silencing of singers in Covid drives Brianna into the shadows where she and a friend meet to engage in the now illicit behavior of singing duets in the woods, where they also grapple with the realities of death, lost community, and the pain of silence.

"A Love Letter to Theatre" by Adarian Sneed, '22, actor

> After COVID forced Adarian to "break up" with acting, she writes an impassioned love letter, pleading that they

might get back together, citing the beautiful and formative experiences they have had together.

"Audition Day" by Sarah Costanza, '24, dancer

In clear detail and candid language, Sarah invites the readers into her head throughout an intense audition, illuminating the emotions, sensations, and significance she feels as a dancer.

"Music and Intention" by Liat Klopouh, '22, pianist

With both humor and candor, Liat explores her life as a diligently trained child-pianist whose resilient parents facilitated her skill and fortitude in ways that challenged her but ultimately opened a world of beauty.

"A Hopeful Confidence" by Whitney Flautt, '23, director

After years of nerves, growth, and a little rejection and reframing, Whitney is inspired to face her fears in a moment of pandemic and uncertainty as she relies on the tools that her experiences as an actor, singer, dancer, choreographer, and eventually director of children's plays have taught her.

"Lens of Admiration" by Grace Powell, '23, photographer

After hearing friends and loved ones doubt themselves, battle depression, and struggle to see beauty in a hurting world, Grace is moved to use photography to draw beauty out of everything she encounters, infusing the world with hope and love however she can.

"The Hardest Performance" by Olivia Blake, '23, EMT

Whether under the pressure of an emergency medicine call, a challenging exam, or a scholarship interview, Olivia's poem explores how chronic overachieving can turn all of life into a performance that can feel hollow and exhausting when she finds herself alone with no life-or-death stakes.

"After Eden" by Mary Costanza, '21, dancer

After years of devotion to ballet, Mary steps back from the stage, first for healing and then because a pandemic closed the studios. In a new posture of reflection, she confesses her struggles, delights in the beauty, and experiences the revelation of how dance became her religion—in some ways she clings to, and in other ways she seeks to embrace. But who is she when she is on the precipice of either losing her religion or sacrificing all else for this faith?

"So the Stones Cry Out" by Ann Phelps, cantor

Whether in the mountains of North Carolina or the cathedrals of Europe, Ann hears her own voice echo back to her with both faith and fear, helping her discover what matters most in her life, especially in moments when clarity is most difficult to discern.

REALIZING HOME

KATHERINE FINCH

It is the first slightly summery-warm day in New York City in months. Every year, this particular first day of warmth and sun is a call to celebration for every New Yorker from every borough. We've made it through the harsh winter months, and we can look forward to a brighter future in the outdoors once again. High school students, like clockwork, cancel their after-school activities and travel to the Great Lawn in Central Park in huge packs. Upon making it to the lawn, they spread out on the grass, gossip, tan, enjoy and spend quality time with their friends.

"Look at them go," I said to my friend Lizzy.

"I know," she replied, "what a concept—having 'after school' free-time." We agreed that we wondered, truly, what it felt like to experience such a sense of freedom to socialize with friends and relax at the end of a school day.

We were standing on the outdoor balcony of the Rose Building at Lincoln Center, the building that houses the Juilliard School, the School of American Ballet, New York City Ballet rehearsal studios, and the Juilliard and School of American Ballet student dormitories and cafeteria. From this spot, we could peer down at these joyful students as they walked with their friends to Central Park on a Friday afternoon. It was 4:00 p.m., which, for a typical high school student, meant the start of the weekend.

For ballerinas, on the other hand, we still had another ballet class to go, perhaps a rehearsal, and then Saturday morning appointments: pilates in the morning, ballet technique class, pointe class, ballroom class, perhaps a music history class, and another rehearsal. Our weekends did not truly begin until Saturday afternoon, and our weekdays did not end until 7:00 p.m. at the earliest. We left our high schools early every day to attend ballet classes, and we were in the studio rain or shine, with complete dedication, and without cancelation. The worst part of my day was the moment when I finally sat down at my desk in my bedroom at 9:00 p.m., exhausted physically and emotionally from the day, yet committed to studying late into the night to pass my academic classes.

The idea of living a normal teenage life always lived in the back of my mind. It was difficult not to compare myself to those of my high school peers who started their homework immediately after school ended at 3:00 p.m. each day, but I knew that I was fortunate enough to be at a ballet school and to study something I was deeply passionate about. While I always daydreamed and fantasized about having a social life and attending parties, there was never a question of whether ballet was *worth it*. I knew it was. I acknowledged that, in the short-term, it would be extremely difficult and taxing, yet I knew that there had to be something I would gain from the experience that would help me in the future. As a result, I put my faith in that feeling and kept at it each and every day, hoping that the *something* I was doing all of this for would reveal itself to me soon.

When I was in a ballet class at the School of American Ballet, I experienced a certain type of magic—an addiction to the feeling of executing a combination to the best of my ability. There was no greater thrill than performing a ballet combination in class and receiving a simple "good, Katherine" from one of my teachers. I fed on that "good" to survive. It was an awful class when I received no affirmation, and it was a terrible day when I did not understand a correction I had received before. That said, the magic came when, after days or weeks of trying to apply a correction, it finally clicked. "*Good*, Katherine! *That's it!*" And that was all I needed. My muscle-memory kicked in, I knew I had improved as a dancer, and my hard work was paying off. I felt like a rockstar or a princess—maybe both.

While discipline and a hard-working nature will always be the primary skills I gained and fine-tuned from my years of ballet training, I gained something significantly more valuable, and for this gift, I would gladly go back and make each sacrifice all over again. I gained an eternal dedication to myself.

Many ballerinas grow up having experienced emotional abuse or a toxic environment, yet I did not. I was fortunate enough to experience an environment in which I received tough love and grew from the experience. At the time, I was a young teenager who grew up at a ballet school and knew nothing other than the diligent ballet-student lifestyle. It would take me until I was in college to realize that the sacrifices I made for an environment that pushed me to always work on myself left its mark on me as a person and global citizen—my personality is based upon a foundation of self-improvement and reflection. I will always have a love of learning new things and advancing my skills because I was trained within that mindset for fifteen years. It will never leave me. It *is* me.

At such a young age, I was forced to work hard and learn the lesson that the decision to sacrifice *now* leads to results *later*. This is not necessarily something that every child is forced to understand until, perhaps, a Friday night in college must be spent studying for an exam rather than out at a social event. These decisions I must make for myself come naturally now as a result of the unique childhood experience I had in the ballet world. For young dancers, ballet training is, in itself, a commitment to dedicate years of sacrifice for a future career. While I chose not to dance professionally, the sacrifices translated, instead, to the future I have chosen off the stage. Wherever I may go in life, I will always value hard work not simply as hard work, but as *self-love*. In other words, I know that the discipline I have is a result of my years of ballet training, and I am unafraid to continue making sacrifices for the person I will be in ten, twenty, or fifty years.

Just last night, in need of a college study break, I pulled into a parking lot to pick up takeout and a milkshake from a new restaurant near Wake Forest. When I pulled in, I found myself facing a small ballet school I never even knew existed. Through the brightly-lit windows, I saw young girls rushing into their pointe class, sewing their ribbons, tightening their buns, and pulling up their tights. Older students were in the studio recalling choreography they were probably about to dance for their ballet teacher. They appeared focused, prepared, and excited to take on the evening of dancing.

I sat there in my car for a minute. The vision brought back all of my fondest memories of dancing. I felt almost as though I had taken a long journey away from home, gotten lost, and finally found home again. I suddenly felt a sense of love and compassion for all of these young dancers, as well as a feeling of empathy for the sacrifices I knew they were making for themselves, just as I once did.

As I peered through the windows as an outsider—now a student with after-school activities and time to tan on the Quad socializing with friends—I realized one thing. The young version of myself who daydreamed about what it would be like to be normal would soon realize that she never would be, regardless of whether she danced or not. As a young ballerina, every day in the studio, and every sacrifice she made, left a permanent mark on her heart.

REALIZING HOME

Forever, no matter what stage of life she is at or how often she dances, she will always be a ballerina. A ballerina is not a dancer, or a student, or even an artist alone. *A ballerina, no matter who she is, is an individual forever designed to love herself by embracing her passions first and foremost.*

These young dancers are only at the beginning. The end I have reached is only the beginning.

I realize now that my ballet journey will never leave me.

I will forever be a ballerina.

WORK IN PROGRESS

LEANNA BERNISH

Am I good at being a girl?

The other girls braid each other's hair. The long, straight tresses belong in their hands. They're woven into dirty blonde patterns of french and fishtail. They are good at being girls. The differing knowledge shimmers between us like a force field. I can do a basic three plait only and have little desire to learn more.

My eyebrows are bushy caterpillars to their thin arches. But isn't Cara Delevingne making thick eyebrows something coveted right now? Frankly I don't want to wax my eyebrows because then I'll be just like the girls who make me feel like I'm the "weird one," the "smart one," the one who doesn't quite get what it means to be a teenage girl. Why would I learn about bronzer and contour when I'm supposed to just like who I am and be okay with that?

But maybe if I did learn, that force field would shatter. Maybe I wouldn't feel so removed as I tug my mouth up and laugh about who said what, even as my gut twinges with the feeling that I'm off-center. Maybe the boys I watch with longing eyes, even though they don't make my heart sing, would think I'm pretty.

I model what the movies and the popular girls with the curated Instagram feeds do. We're 14, and everyone is prettier than me.

They're prettier than you.

I ask my friends, "Why do you get it, and I don't?"

"You're intimidating. Maybe that's why the boys don't go for you. I mean, don't change that; it's good that you know who you are," they say.

But it hurts to be who you are when that means people can't relate to you and have no interest in dating you.

***

Acrylic paint is scary.

Especially for a detail-orientated, cautious person such as myself. It is not easily controlled, and as a sophomore in high school who has only done two acrylic pieces before, I don't know what I'm doing yet. I paint tentatively, watering the pigment down so much that, in the end, my piece resembles one of watercolor rather than acrylic. Gradually, I learn to water down my paints less. This is thanks to my own growing confidence and the support of my art teacher and my two good friends. They encourage me to have faith in my abilities and foray outside of my comfort zone.

Blob that paint onto the canvas. Mix dark reds and blues for shadows. Believe in yourself.

Bolstered by their words, I find my love of impressionism.

Achieving great realism through the expression of light and frenetic brushstrokes, impressionism creates an antithetical structure that I adore. I accept that hyperrealism doesn't have to be the goal every time. In my use of globs and globs of paint and short, quick, dancing brushstrokes, I find peace. I am no longer obsessing over every shadow, every pore. I'm just painting. I feverishly work when I stumble upon a good shade or technique, the spirit of fleeting mastery possessing my hand for a few moments. I strive for

WORK IN PROGRESS

that euphoric feeling. The world becomes rose-tinted, and nothing else exists but my brush and my canvas.

As I have gained a newfound appreciation for the numerous possibilities of acrylic paint when uninhibited by my own fear, I have found a love for the dynamic nature of light. The warmth of golden hour, the way it turns everyone and everything orange in the best way possible. The fluorescent diner lighting of a Clemmons Dairio which imbues the ordinary with the reverence of a Hopper painting: captivating nighthawks at a dark, wood counter. The natural light softly whispering through the opaque glass window of the Reynolds High School Auditorium bathroom.

***

One winter day in 2020, I dug my flannel pj pants out from storage where they'd grown dusty with disuse during the fall semester. I queued up my CDs for the day. I felt the itch to create. I pulled out an old piece of watercolor paper, still taped to cardboard by the hopes of an imagined project long gone. Like a varsity athlete returning to their high school track, I shook out the joints with a light wash. I did dynamic stretches with each added layer of color. I found my youth again as I took a curve with ease into the homestretch, creating a finished piece of vibrant hues.

Seven blissful hours later I had a technicolor watercolor of the Wake Radio studio.

Making art used to be scary. My perfectionist standards loomed large. They still have a presence, but I stand toe-to-toe with them now. Part of my hesitancy to begin or work on a piece stems from years of pressure I've placed on myself to uphold my own exceptional standards and those of the people I cannot disappoint. I fear I won't be able to live up to myself. Yet once I get going and tap into my artist self, my right brain activates muscle memory.

I am learning to trust in what I've done before. Take a hike, left brain! I will appreciate everything I make, no matter the "flaws."

The creation of the last piece of my senior art concentration birthed this new thinking. My original idea wasn't clicking. It was the beginning of quarantine, and I missed my friends terribly. Who knew when I'd see them again? As I sat in our front room abundant with daylight, as I was wont to do in those days, I was hit with the idea of a piece full of color and wavy lines – very 70s. I needed to create with joy and freedom. No strict, gridded paper for this project. We would spell out "Hello" in ASL, connected by those wavy lines to illustrate how we could still communicate by phone. Each friend was drawn in their own specific color, either their favorite or the one I associate with them. The space and freedom I gave myself to think allowed me to create something free of external expectations, something which became one of my favorites of high school.

If creating for art class was my snug pair of mom jeans that are only good for the work day, creating "Hello" was that favorite pair of well-worn, lumberjack plaid, flannel pajama pants. I don't mind the jeans. But I grin and do a little dance as I put on my flannel pj pants. Every part of my body relaxes as I slip those on, just as my mind settles more comfortably into itself when creating "Hello." This ease allowed me to explore sketching next. The drawings became unattached, unencumbered by judgment and comparisons to past work. I could appreciate them simply for what they were, flaws included. Sketching in this way became an extension of journaling: a means to reflect, to brain dump.

Making art is not scary. It is a catalyst for joy. It is an old friend, one I can fall right back into laughter with, no matter how long it's been since we've seen each other.

WORK IN PROGRESS

Using makeup does not have to mean fear and comparison. It can be the new friend who I feel like I've known my entire life. When I was 14, I saw makeup as a compromise, a begrudging acquiescence to something and someone whom I didn't want to be. It was a catch-22. Be like them and be inducted. Be myself and stay true to my center. The oscillation between the two blurred my sense of self into an uncomfortable ambiguity.

Then came the summer before senior year.

The summer when I learned to see myself as a canvas free from my own judgment.

The summer when the ambiguity became a whole new palette of grays to be explored.

The summer of wild, curly hair so unlike those straight, blonde tresses. The summer of bright eyes, confident waves to any kind, cute boy, and dazzling smiles.

I wore what I wanted to. I didn't stand in front of the mirror long enough to let the negativity creep in and decompose the self I had built for the day.

I found tranquility in the silence that replaced the internal cacophony of familiar comparison. The cacophony I had fostered like a devilish plant, with witch-finger branches that tore away at my self-image piece by piece. I began to dress how I wanted to. With each new day, I pulled out a root, until all that was left was fresh soil where I planted the joyous blooms of denim shorts, braless outfits, and light makeup.

I didn't have to have a full face of makeup to be pretty. Eyebrows and mascara. Art socks and mom jeans. Bam. Happy. I could be me, and everyone else could be themselves. My roommate and friends held my new approach to identity high up above their heads, giving me the opportunity to crowd surf on their support.

I could be gorgeous and smart.

No hierarchy existed to tell me otherwise or to shove me into a rickety throne in the royal court's shadow. I was surrounded at all times by beautiful people who were unapologetically themselves. We were all entities coexisting and learning from each other, seeing the beauty we each offered in our own ways. Learning to grow comfortable in these new fashions and face paint was the stepping stone to the desire I now hold to paint my eyes in green, yellow or *Own Ur Power* lavender.

***

April 15, 2020. A month into quarantine.

My days were infused with a simplicity and curiosity I had not experienced since I was 11 years old in a brand-new house without internet. On this particular day the urge to "create a whole look despite having nowhere to take it" was especially strong. I was pulled to my one bag of makeup by a gravitational tug in my center – the heroine on the precipice of her coming-of-age quest. I pulled out my singular eyeshadow palette and dug around in my memories like a woman searching through her overcrowded purse for Tic-Tacs. I closed my hand around the memory of the time my dear, makeup guru friend taught me how to do eye shadow. I opened my 8-color palette, shuffling color combinations in my head like Sherlock Holmes. I daubed a solid amount of the lightest shade onto the inside halves of my eyelids, the almost watercolor, acrylic wash covering the canvas. I pulled the darker hue from the outside in, arcing over the curve of my eye. The cobalt blue and burnt sienna Liquitex paint for depth. I blended the two together with a shiny, middle hue. The unaltered white paint, my go-to blender. I created a look which made my dad puzzle, "Your eyes are orange," and made me feel like Padmé Amidala: powerful.

A full look didn't suddenly become an everyday thing; I still did just brows and mascara or no makeup most days. Yet every so often my singular non-black Colourpop eyeliner, buried at the bottom of my burlap makeup bag for years before, glazed my eyelids with honey butter. I experimented with my 8-color palette, adding pink depths of flower centers. Not too long after, I found myself scrolling through Colourpop and Glossier's websites in daydreams of dewy, colorful eyeliners and Prismacolor eyeshadow palettes. Through social media and my own convincing, I was seeing art as something for the wearer, not the observers.

I wanted to explore this new method of painting. My family heard me. For Christmas they gave me Colourpop galore. An Urban Decay palette appropriately titled "Born to Run," covered in images of travel and adventure, more wanderlust for a college freshman. I felt the feeling any artist knows, familiar to our bones. That pricking in your fingers. That lighting of your eyes as you envision the endless potential beheld in front of you. We know how to make whole worlds out of pots of palette no bigger than quarters.

My acrylic paint tubes, bent like modern dancers from many a project, and my brushes, few but sturdy, splattered with the excess of many an impassioned marathon painting session, have been replaced for the time being. Their current counterparts are cloudscape and flower field eyeshadow palettes, petal soft, yet Basquiat bright. The occasionally shaken off, but not washed, Target makeup brush set. Doing my makeup brings me back to the simplicity of sidewalk chalk. You spend your time creating a masterpiece, only to have it worn down by car tires and washed away completely by the rain. The day's look is gradually eroded by the eye rubbing and temple scratching of studying and springtime allergies. It washes away forever in the evening's lukewarm, hot on a good day, shower in Angelou Residence Hall. I know no look will last, but each is beautiful in its embrace of the present. It is a true illustration of the temporary nature of things, especially given my tendency to forget eyeshadow primer.

Just as one can envision a painting as big as a museum wall from five tubes of paint and some brushes, I am able to see myself in the worlds of makeup and femininity. I am finding belonging in my interpretations of these worlds, for knowing how to fishtail braid and do bronzer are not the only ways to be a girl.

My femininity is my black, flare mom jeans. My white, 80s Vans which are no longer pristine but have "character." My yellow, crew Gustav Klimt socks and matching eyeshadow. My climber's build which allows me to pull myself up a wall on a hold no deeper than the width of a dime. My curves I use to dance to 2000s pop and Dua Lipa like no one's business.

I'm good at being a girl.

I'm good at being me.

BREATHBORN(E)

BRIANNA COPPOLINO

Musicians are accustomed to rejection but

The fear is new

When did my brother's trumpet become

A loaded gun

And I, the songstress, a dire wyrm, disgorging

Miasma in place of melody

Our air is laced with blight

But our art is sewn of breath

Thus, the audience shies and shrivels

The fields we tended fleeing from the scythe

Lest we reap them with our strain

No rain of applause floods these empty concert halls

And the drought in our coffers compels the desert swell

Where might have bloomed

The flower of delight

Brianna Coppolino

We mill about our crystal labyrinth of screens

Between us webs of windows plucking

Voices from the air

And air from the voices

Till they are naught but dry, windless static

Music, spun unfiltered, billows damp and fertile

Balmy clouds to burgeon and condense

Where lips and hands should kiss and glide

As body, heart, and mind in sacred union sing

Now, somehow, what we touch we taint

With the waters of our bellows

No device may aptly translate the timbre of those streams

Thus, the screens must dam and damn us

To desiccation in solitude

Caged birds wear clothespins on their beaks

And muffled cries pass softly through the bars

Perhaps these once were songs before

The cover descended and remained

Too long shrouded in their dreary cotton cloisters

Some birds believe the world has ended

BREATHBORN(E)

Yet, the sun crawls quietly onwards

Holding its breath

And my meadowlark mother hums

Guten morgen sonnenschein

So she may believe

The morning is good

Dawn breaks and musicians die

As they have always died

Brittle bones rotting like the heartwood

Of some aged or afflicted oak

We fall, though none perceive the cadence

For the forest is deaf

And the hills, asleep

Those solemn final chords resound

Though heedless earth offers no echo

Its gaping streets are stalked by wary strangers

In the faded footprints

Of marching saints

A pianist who swung from cradle to casket

Will not receive his jazz funeral

Brianna Coppolino

Only emails to drown the lacrimal chorus

Today's gospel is from Phobos, 20:20

Fear thy neighbor

And breathe not as ye pass them

For the air of the tomb shall rise from their throat

And doom your heart to stillness

Word of god, word of life

Death may be breathborne but so are words

And silence is another grave

We are entombed within ourselves

The air beneath our ribs left to stagnante and peutrify

There is a scent of despair and it lingers

In the voiceless draft behind my mask

I stare at other singers from the safety of my aviary

To wonder what unsung corpses

Decompose on their lips

Still, a grain of verve persists

Though clandestinely pursued

I've been told my evening rendezvous appear arcane

And reek of creeping devilry

BREATHBORN(E)

Gathered witches in the wood

She and I traversing mire and bramble

Where young copperheads might coil

That our voices, paired, may waft across the marsh

In misty incantation

Conjuring visions born of breath and joy

Pur ti miro, pur ti godo, pur ti stringo

Our vapors intertwine as amorous serpents

Their counterpoint to shift aside coagulate debris Tepid spirits, now aflow

To serve this tenderest of bacchanals

At last, we drink and, in her verse

I taste felicity

Both overture and requiem

We sing, unmasked, undamed, uncaged

Unafraid, partaking in the pleasures

Of forbidden harmony

Should one follow this lilting line

To find us in the springing rite

Would they see our duet bound and burned

Brianna Coppolino

For daring to disturb the sleeping hills

And in an ariose stream

Flush ash from the sealed ear of the forest

Her witchcraft resurrected me

Took hold of my clay vessel

To banish tarnish and decay

And o'er its open lip she poured her own berceuse

Più non peno, più non moro

There is a scent of hope and it lingers

In the breath between us

A LOVE LETTER TO THEATRE

ADARIAN SNEED

I perform for me. I perform for you.

I perform for our past, present, and future.

But most of all I perform for the memories. The memories that I make and take home with me, the memories we make together that you can take home with you.

There is magic in those memories.

So I go back to the stage again and again so I can continue that production of memories.

Dear Theatre,

I'm just going to say it. I miss you. Remember that first encounter when we were singing the ABC song during the preschool recital? I was so comfortable with being vulnerable with you on stage. So much so that I screamed "A B C D E F G..." at the top of my lungs. I had more confidence and charisma, and that was only our first date. Though it was early in our relationship, I didn't even have to question it. From that moment on, you became the love of my life.

Remember when we were just 5 years old? So young and so open to all the possibilities the world had to offer us. Montclair, NJ, was so beautiful. People from all walks of life come to live in this town. We were happy there. We were so invested in one another. A year never went by where there wasn't an opportunity to be engaged in acting, singing, dancing, performing—all the things that made our relationship so strong. I remember in school, before we were official, there were others interested in you. They were young and wanted to be in the plays and productions too. However, as time went on, most of them began to fade away. They gained interest in other activities. But I stayed. I continued to be involved with you straight through elementary, middle, high school, and now college. When contemplating whether or not I should continue with our relationship after high school, I was faced with inner conflict. I asked myself, "What am I really doing when I'm up there on that stage?" When I think about other relationships, I consider what they give to the world. Water and sunlight give life to a plant. Salt and pepper bring us flavor and spice. A song and a dance give each other a true purpose. So what does a performer and theatre give to the world? What do we give to the world, my love?

I love you. I loved you. I still love you. I believe people are put in your life for a reason. You were put in my life for a reason. You bring things out of me that I otherwise would not be able to tap into. Especially when it comes to song, emotions on stage, and my meaningful movement throughout space. However, the main reason you were put in my life is so together we could provide others with an escape. Life is hard: plain and simple. Every day we hear about death, human rights injustices, violence, financial strains, discrimination, and the list goes on. I believe that you, Theatre, provide people with a moment of escape while also giving them the tools to deal with reality. When sitting in a theatre, experiencing a live show for two hours, there is absolutely nothing to do but sit, focus, and enjoy the performance. Once the two hours are over, people can be reinvigorated to go back and

A LOVE LETTER TO THEATRE

continue with the inevitability that life is. We can't ignore what life throws at us, but we can find ways to maneuver through it. You, Theatre, keep us maneuvering through life. I came to this realization about us when we had that talk about our love languages. It allowed me to see that being on stage wasn't just about what I received from it, but rather what I was able to give to the world through theatre, through you. The answer is: I give it through memories.

Because at this moment, the memories are all we have.

I don't know if you remember this, but when I was in the 5th grade, I was so shy that I didn't enjoy being in large group settings. But that did not stop me from loving one large group setting in particular. The stage. Little Adarian seemed to become a whole different person on stage. Over the years, my family was so supportive of us and sat back as they watched me blossom. You know, being on the stage develops a sense of power and confidence. You may remember this, but I'll just tell you again. It's one of those moments that really showed me how I've grown as a person while being with you. The memory took place at the 5th grade talent show. I was singing "Everything's Coming Up Roses." I had gotten through two verses, but my full performance consisted of three. My second verse ended on this comforting high note that triggered the audience to think my performance was over. They began clapping and cheering. I was so thankful for the applause that I didn't want to do anything that seemed like I was ungrateful. I remembered looking out into the audience and smiling. Then I confidently said something along the lines of "thank you and one more." This made the audience laugh to see this 11-year-old girl claim her stage! It is a memory that pops up in my mind. Does it pop up in yours? For me, it's one of those memories that makes me smile when trying to get through tough times. Does it make you smile anymore?

It is our memories that make us who we are. And it is important to remember that not all of ours have been positive. Some memories are difficult if not painful. But from that pain is usually a lesson. We were preparing to play the Witch in *Into the Woods*. This part was so extravagant that it was set to be the peak of my theatrical career. A great deal of preparation had to go into this show in order for it to exist in a space of truth and authenticity. The most challenging aspect of playing the role was the amount of vocal range that is required. It calls for someone with a deep voice that feels almost like they are hugging you when they sing. While at the same time a higher voice draws your attention with how smooth and simple it is. In all honesty, I struggled to find this balance.

I remember being in the designer run for *Woods* and singing "Last Midnight." It is one of the most iconic songs of the Witch and coincidently the peak of her character arc. Singing the song was physically draining. I remember getting to the final lyric of the song which is a half-sung, half-screamed "CRUNCH." Singing this note pained me. I truly felt like something so sharp and so rigid was slowly ripping down my throat. This was a painful moment emotionally and physically, so I naturally learned something from it. One: that I shouldn't ever feel like I have to push myself to make something great. The second thing I learned was to communicate. You by nature are so collaborative, yet I was so focused on the individualistic aspect of me and me alone. I needed to communicate with you more about what felt right and what didn't. And I know you would have been right there supporting me. This is a moment where we grew. Thank God for memories because this is one I won't forget; it's one that I can't forget.

Even now, when the memories are all we have.

I'm just going to say it. We've grown too far apart. These memories we've shared simply won't leave my mind. The reason I think we

A LOVE LETTER TO THEATRE

should get back together is to create more of these memories. The world smiles when we thrive together. We were together and made memories for so many years. I have always been in a show, in a theatre, and in the process of bonding with a cast of people. I must say that for a while I haven't known what life is like when these things are not going on, without you being a constant in my life. So, you might understand just how shocking it was when it all came to a halt. In 2020, when we broke up, I was challenged. For me, there is something so magical about the brief relationship between the performer and an audience member in live theatre. By not having our magic, I realized just how deeply rooted you are in the fabric of my life. So, I write this letter to you to say I want you back. I crave what was once familiar, comforting, and magical. I long to make more memories, remembering how happy we were at just five years old, how much we grew, and how much we still have to offer the world together.

So, will you take me back, my love? If so, meet me in front of the box office. Our favorite spot where we can see if we can rekindle our love for making memories yet again.

Love,

Adarian

AUDITION DAY

SARAH COSTANZA

Audition days as a ballet dancer are always fraught with nerves. Whether the audition is for a role in a production you have dreamed of or a simple level placement in your studio does not matter; the nerves are the same. The night before the audition, from the moment I lay my head on my pillow to the moment I wake after a fitful night of tossing and turning, it is the sole thing occupying my mind. I've spent hours lying awake, stewing over the possibilities and worrying about the outcome of the next day. Bright and early, when my alarm sounds and my eyes open, it rushes to my mind—the realization that it is the day that has loomed before me for weeks. The pressure mounts, and I take a deep breath to try and expel it. I remind myself that all I can do is try my hardest, prepare well, and let my years of hard work show in my performance.

The weeks leading up to the audition have been filled with extra hours in the studio, pushing myself to be better and hone my technique to as near perfection as I am able to attain. For those few weeks, the barre had become my home, and the music the very air I breathed. My focus shifts solely to my goal, and it occupies the front of my mind. It is because of this that I am able to wake today and push away the nerves. I know that I have given it my all. If I am to be disappointed by the result of the audition, I can find solace in the fact that I've put my best foot forward and pushed myself to the limit.

Sarah Costanza

After waking and taking a moment to collect my thoughts to prepare for the day, I climb out of bed and begin my usual morning routine. The simplicity of the familiar routine calms me. I brush my teeth, wash my face, and then head into the kitchen for some much-needed coffee. I pair my coffee with a light breakfast of avocado toast and fruit. Fuelled and caffeinated, I return to my room.

I begin by meticulously applying my makeup. Auditions always call for a little extra to help you stand out and bolster your confidence. After brushing on all the needed pigments and coating my lashes in dark mascara, I begin the process of wrapping my hair into a tight and sturdy ballet bun. A ballet bun is different from other buns in that it must be extremely secure so as to ensure that it will not fall out once I begin dancing. I brush through my hair, mist it with water, and slick it back to secure it into a ponytail at the crown of my head. Once I am positive my ponytail is tight enough to be secure, I separate my hair into different strands and twist them into the shape of a bun and meticulously pin them down with hairpins. With the addition of a hairnet and a generous coat of hairspray, my bun is complete, and I knew that I can rely on it to last the day.

Feeling presentable, I then select my favorite leotard that I feel the most confident in from my closet and change into my leotard and tights. I pile on warm-up gear and move to the floor to begin stretching and loosening my muscles for the day. My routine involves beginning by rolling out my muscles with a foam roller, doing some light body conditioning, then finishing with some gentle stretches. Knowing my right achilles tendon has shortened and swelled with tendonitis, I give it particular care, ensuring it won't betray me. Once I feel I am adequately limber, I gather my things into my dance bag: my flat and pointe shoes, an extra pair of tights and leotard, a can of hairspray, extra warm-up gear, and any other items I think I may need for the day. Sure that I have everything I need, I clamber into my car and drive to the North Carolina School of the Arts.

The studio is only two hours away, but I always leave early enough to ensure that I make it to the audition at least an hour early. To me, it is imperative that I show up with enough time to get my bearings and warm-up prior to the start of the audition. If I know that I have adequate time to prepare, I feel much calmer and ready when the time comes for the audition to begin.

Upon walking into the studio where the audition is held, I am instantly met with the chatter of my fellow auditioners. One would think that walking into the room to meet your competition would increase your nerves tenfold, but I have found that it has the opposite effect on me. When I enter the room to find everyone talking amongst themselves, it reminds me that beyond each other's competition, we are a group of people with an incredible amount in common, and we all feel the exact same way. To me, there is an abundance of comfort in that. Witnessing everyone getting to know each other, chatting in corners while hoisting their legs over their heads, helps me to see it as a much more amicable environment and helps lessen my nerves.

Once in the studio, I find a free spot to place my bag and begin warming up while talking to the girls around me. These conversations offer a great distraction from the nervous thoughts that would have otherwise plagued me. Slowly, the time until the audition winds down, and I finish my warm-ups. I am called into the audition room, and rather paradoxically, a sense of calm washes over me. Because a ballet class is the place where I feel the most comfortable and sure of myself.

I have been a ballet dancer for almost 15 years. The methodic routine of a ballet class is something ingrained in every muscle fiber of my body. Once I am in a class, I can turn on autopilot and let my body do what it knows how to do without a second thought. I make it through the audition this way, with confidence in my abilities and the knowledge that giving it my all is enough.

At the end of any audition, I am almost always filled with a sense of pride. Whether I believe I did well or poorly, I am always proud of the fact that I tried my best and had the courage to put myself out there and be vulnerable.

And then, relief.

The knowledge that the final decision is out of my hands and that my role in the process is now over is somehow liberating. I know that the results of the audition will come, but I also know that the results are not a reflection of who I am as a person. They are simply someone else's opinion of how well I performed in one class and are incapable of measuring my value or worth. I get back in my car and drive down I-74 to Southern Pines, North Carolina, and step back into my day, now anxiety free, ready to return to normal life.

MUSIC AND INTENTION

LIAT KLOPOUH

To recreate a piece of classical music is to unlock a capsule of emotion buried deep in the score before you.

It is to bring the work to life, stretching the imagination as far as it will go, giving way to a balance of narratives. It's this emotion that probes your own, that lets you humanize the score and embody the composer's story. You may find yourself losing sight of your surroundings, falling into an artistic trance, taken back to centuries past when its creation was underway. But as you focus on illuminating the pain, the anger, the frustration, and the joy through those chiming keys, you may find yourself feeling more focused and centered than before.

***

The piano and I have a history.

We met when I was four years old, barely able to reach the halfway point between the bench and the floor, much less the pedals. I guess that's the beauty of the instrument; you can learn to give it life without needing to match its size or its strength. Like most kids, I resented playing for a long time before growing to love it. But that didn't sway my parents from obligating daily practice. Silenced throughout their own childhood as Jews growing up in Soviet Russia, freedom of self-expression—no matter what medium it came in—was a privilege in and of itself; there was no excuse to let such an opportunity slip through my fingers.

Seated uncomfortably upon that bench, my stubborn four-year-old self could never have imagined the gratitude I would one day feel for their insistence and diligence.

In the seventh grade, I remember desperately wanting to spend the summer at sleepaway camp. Predictably, the idea was utterly foreign to my parents. It didn't make the slightest sense to *want* to sleep away from home. More importantly, to go without practicing piano for two months was out of the question. The final compromise was a performing arts camp in the middle of Sweden, Maine. I would be majoring in piano and minoring in voice, practicing every day, learning to sight-read faster, and working with esteemed mentors. Every kid's dream. As my friends prepared for waterparks and volleyball tournaments, I was sorrowfully printing sheets of music to work through and perfect by August.

Yet isn't it often the case that our best experiences manifest when we least expect them to? Slowly learning that I had a knack for the piano, I grew to love and appreciate it. The people I was surrounded by, students and mentors alike, were not only warm and welcoming but incredibly talented. I was acquainted with kids from all walks of life, all races, ethnicities, and religions, and all connected by a pure and raw love for music and its history. As the summer ran its course, I found myself unexpectedly captivated by the uses of color in Chopin's Four Ballades, by the irony of Mahler's First Symphony, and the hints of melancholy in Brahms' Cello Sonata. I remember the first time I heard George Gershwin's "Rhapsody in Blue"—it was like watching smooth chocolate pouring out of a ramekin.

Confidence was never my strong suit. Gratuitously shy as a kid,

MUSIC AND INTENTION

anxious to engage, and slow to digest conversation, I always felt behind in a world that worships charisma and poise.

Developing a voice, fully honest and true to myself, has been a challenging feat in the presence of self-criticism, judgment, and doubt. I've been told this kind of self-acceptance and assurance is not something that can be taught, but rather learned through experience and perhaps gradually with age. It's funny how often this advice rings true as I discover, engage, and connect with new interests, beginning that summer with music. At the piano, I found that voice, and it continues to sing with certainty and conviction, telling a story better than I can with my own words.

***

When I sat down to practice, I did it with intention.

Alongside my own, the voice of my summer mentor stays with me in the memories of our lessons and conversations. We'd begin in silence, listening—really listening—to a recording of the piece I'd been grappling with. Sometimes we'd focus on the breathtaking; other times, we'd lament the mundane, or perhaps we'd deliberate the performer's directional changes in the music. We'd talk about history: not only the composer's but the performer's as well. Many pianists, I learned, connect with and relate to a particular composer above all others, a connection that inevitably comes through in the music.

"Pressing keys mechanically won't get you far," this mentor would say. "You have to know and *feel* what you're doing on the inside." I came to understand that to convey a story meaningfully and influence the hearts and minds of an audience requires more from us as performers than mere knowledge and memorization of the score. It involves a kind of inner commitment: a genuine understanding and willingness to embody the music before us.

With nowhere to be and nowhere to go in the middle of Sweden, Maine, I'd sit in a small, cramped, and pungent practice room, windows open to let the breeze in. The serenity of the woods made the air feel peaceful; it was a blank canvas gradually shaded with the color of trumpets, violins, and cellos in the practice rooms nearby. With hours to spend, I started identifying individual sections to work on and reflected on the particulars of each page. I learned to practice consciously and with genuine focus. Even the way my body leaned into the keyboard would affect the softness of the keys. I was using all five senses to make the music sing, to unlock that capsule of emotion. And as I took the smallest steps in progress each day, I seemed to be gaining more and more control of the instrument. Despite difficult technical passages, I centered that focus, and I practiced intentionally.

***

Only recently has the piano become a guiding hand for me.

At the onset of Covid, I did what many of us had to do to keep our sanity—or perhaps what classically trained pianists have been habituated to do—creating a strict routine to keep myself from thinking too deeply about world events. Indeed, it alleviated some of the anxiety I seemed to share with the rest of the nation. Tangible goals and a predictable schedule tend to keep us fairly stable in a time that is anything but predictable.

Slowly, however, I found myself treating that routine as though it was a lifeline. With no human contact and no socialization, I was completing tasks merely to get them finished and out of the way. There was little meaning to coursework, as seasonal goals slipped away with every passing month that the pandemic loomed. I found myself confronted with an empty schedule and complying with empty rules. Now, after a year of Zoom, classes that I once would

MUSIC AND INTENTION

have approached with inordinate enthusiasm and zest, I struggle to sit through. Papers that once would have been intriguing to write and meditate over, I find to be a burden. Learning and writing, the two things I valued above all else coming into college, have both become a chore to complete. For the past year, I realize I've been moving through life mechanically and senselessly: following the schedule, the plan. But in the midst of all of it, I lost genuine curiosity and, more importantly, genuine presence.

Now, as I reflect on those pure and slow-moving childhood summers, I'm beginning to recall and appreciate the role that intention plays in a life of meaning and purpose. Perhaps we don't all have the freedom to lessen our loads, but we do have the opportunity to cultivate that same presence and mindfulness we used to nurture as children. In these deliberate times, I often find myself clutching those nostalgic memories of breezy Maine summers, worn-down wooden keys, and the familiar feeling of enthusiasm at the site of a new score.

As the world recalibrates normalcy, we are being thrown back into the fast-paced and competitive cycle we were forced to break free of last March. But after a year of moving senselessly from task to task, I am learning from those people in my life who have abandoned that race in order to breathe, reflect and re-evaluate. In my final year of college, I challenged myself to revitalize that love of learning that I held on to so firmly before the pandemic; to be more engaged, more mindful, and more committed to things I take on. I challenge myself to listen better, to be more present in my relationships. And I challenge myself to welcome responsibility, following through on it intentionally.

From what I've learned over these past seventeen years of growth as a musician, it is only through a steadfast dedication and sincere focus to even the most mundane of tasks that we can become grateful for our achievements and clearer in our vocation.

***

To grow with a piece of classical music is to let it be shaped and molded by your development and experience.

It is to understand that art can be transformed and re-interpreted, even if only in our minds. For the performer, it is to remember that every piece has a new lesson to offer, a new message to convey, and a new way to connect with it. Growing with a piece of classical music involves revision, and re-orientation with every experience, both in the score and in ourselves. In this season of solitude and separation, music can bring us into a relationship with the creator, can revive the audiences that cannot congregate, and can draw us into deeper relationships with ourselves.

A HOPEFUL CONFIDENCE

WHITNEY FLAUTT

The dimming lights cued my entry. I wiped my sweaty palms against my cloak, against each other, and against my cloak again. The particles tingled on my hands as my heart raced as fast as my mind. "Am I good enough to share the stage with these professional performers?" I asked myself. I inhaled deeply and my throat strained to relax on the exhale. I hear someone in the orchestra offer the opening note—a C—and begin proceeding down the aisle with my basket. My feet seem to float through the air while my chest contracts under pressure. I make eye contact with those whom I pass to see eyes full of hope, excitement, and just a touch of judgment. My knees shake as I climb the stairs to the stage, and I engage my core to stay vertical. I engage with the other cast members as we set the stage, though my mind runs through the coming movements. My fellow singers mention a dance. All eyes fall to me. I gasp for a breath beneath my plastered smile only to choke on the air. I pass off my basket and walk to center stage. Relying on my many hours of training, I stepped silently onto center stage and forced my arms into port de bra. Hearing the violins, flutes, and piano, I lose myself in the music, letting the instrumental staccato initiate my movements. Instinct takes over from there until the music fades, and I finished my solo with an uncontrollable smile and magical confidence. I realize in this moment that, no matter a person's age or experience, the stage can dissipate insecurities and boost confidence.

Showing up to an audition always took an immense amount of courage. As I grew up dancing in my studio from the age of 3, my teachers cast all of the shows. I was secure in their perception of my skill level. I would therefore enter an audition in a protective cloud, free to move. As an eighth grader, I decided to expand my realm, trying my hand at acting. The spring before I even completed middle school, I threw myself into a high school drama program full of experienced older students whom I had never met. Without having seriously acted before, my stomach and jaw simultaneously dropped when the director divided us into pairs, instructing us to perform an opening scene together. With five minutes to prepare with an older actor who had infinitely more experience, I willed my feet to keep from running out the door. I lost all sense of being as I could not process anything my partner said in those five minutes. I looked at their hands, feet, and lips moving but nothing registered. I strained to open my eyes after each blink. I sat down to collect myself and tried to slow my heartbeat which began to pound in my ears. As my heart-rate slowed in my ears and throat, I felt my body-shakes subside. Hearing my name called, I opened my eyes and authoritatively took center stage. I relied on my instincts and put my own spin on the character, even making the director chuckle. Then he instructed us to change roles and play the other. My eyebrows shot up, and my whole body convulsed into a tense state. I had only memorized my part. I had only memorized my part. Mind racing, I began saying the other line. Halfway through, silence rang through the room as I knew I had the next line but had no idea what words came next. My voice croaked out a sound, unable to form actual words, echoing back the sound of a frog. My partner whispered the next line to me, and with their help, I completed the scene. I finished. The teamwork I experienced that day allowed me to realize the community that performing requires.

A HOPEFUL CONFIDENCE

Even amidst my new community and growing comfort as an actor, performing grew challenging in high school. Constant comparisons threatened to take over the support I had encountered, clouding my theatre community. Like my peers, I considered seniority to be a factor in casting. Nonetheless, as I got older, my roles remained the same. I stayed a part of the chorus in musicals and remained on stage for all of five minutes in the plays. I worked with coaches and teachers both in and out of my school's department to improve my acting and singing. My sophomore year, I decided to focus on acting because it brought me more joy and left more room to discover self-expression. After 14 years of dancing daily, I quit dance to make time for drama rehearsals and extra practice. However, even with the extra dedication, I fell short of scoring a bigger role. What was I doing? Who was I becoming? Yet I kept coming back, developing humility and the capacity to gauge my skill set, seeing that dancing and supporting others allowed me to thrive.

During my junior year, I worked with the choreographer who previously noticed my natural memorization and execution of new choreography to establish a new position: dance captain. I served in this role until graduation. I was a member of the chorus but ran extra rehearsals to clean and run all dance numbers. Every day after rehearsal, a smile would emerge on my face when I would see the light click as a new dancer retained a different piece of the choreography. The cast benefited greatly from the extra practice, and I maintained my dance skills through learning and teaching all of the numbers in the show, even when I was not in them. The choreographer was so pleased with the cleaned numbers that she granted me the responsibility of choreographing two of my own, further instilling my sense of purpose on the stage.

I used this newfound passion for teaching as I volunteered to produce and direct the children's play *Rumpelstiltskin* at the local

Boys and Girls Club. We worked for three months on the show as I introduced them to the audition and rehearsal processes. At showtime, half of my cast of fourth grade actors told me they were too nervous to speak. Recognizing their fear, I held their hands and instructed them to close their eyes.

"Go back to rehearsal. Picture me in the audience and no one else," I said.

I nudged each of them gently on-stage. They entered with their shoulders by their ears and began the scene with muffled voices. I made eye contact with the child playing

Rumpelstiltskin and smiled. Her eyes narrowed and the corners of her mouth perked. My heart fluttered as I watched her enter boldly: shoulders down and chest lifted high. Her voice matched her stance, and her castmates fed off of her energy. Joy filled the stage and the room as the entire atmosphere shifted with each burst of laughter. Bounding off the stage to applause, they gave me NBA-worthy high fives, and I knew they had tasted and relished the glory of the stage! Somehow, my years of reflection and diligent work had allowed me to find the place where my discovered confidence, humility, and resilience could help others in my community thrive as well.

Watching Covid disable the performing industry ignites me with fear. Performing has brought me so much joy, but performing virtually does not give you the same connection with an audience or fellow cast and crew members. Music and dance have given me a way to express myself, manage my anxiety, conquer adolescent insecurities, and boost my confidence. Performance affords the opportunity to communicate effectively and share my passions and beliefs in a highly personalized way. In a virtual setting, there is no way to feed off of the audience's energy. Live theatre calls for a level of preparation and perfection, however no live performance is ever the same. There is an art that coincides with the interconnectivity between that cast and audience.

There is mutual trust and an established relationship.

As the music fades, the audience rises in abounding applause. I curtsey left and right as the corners of my mouth rise into a smile. My heart races to match the beat of their claps. I have found my community. One that creates a warm environment in the auditorium, unable to be recreated through a screen.

LENS OF ADMIRATION

GRACE POWELL

"Grace, I am going to get a nose job."

Her words pierced through the air we were both breathing, and we noticed a new shift in heaviness around us. It took me more than a second to process what I had just heard.

I was sitting across from this beautiful woman with eyes that are like melting chocolate and noticed the light highlighting the perfectly ornate detail of her face and hair. As I looked into her eyes, I realized that she was serious and believed that somehow she wasn't enough, exactly as she was, in that moment.

All I wanted to do was change her mind and convince her that she didn't need any alterations. I longed to free her from this cage of lies she was stuck in, but the level of complete certainty in her voice left me completely speechless. How do you argue with such certainty, rooted in years of quiet yet destructive lies, that you aren't enough? Instead, I just sat across from her and tried to listen to her reasonings and justifications. After that conversation, I took note of the disconnect between how I saw her and how she saw herself. It left an instantaneous imprint—a photographic negative of her perspective, the opposite of what she saw in herself. Where she saw flaws, I saw beauty. And in that moment, as quick as the opening and the closing of the camera's shutter that somehow captures a whole world with its flash, a memory worth a thousand words came back to me.

***

Last year, my friend Anna asked me to photograph her for her last year of high school—a true honor to memorialize such a momentous occasion. As we were planning a morning to do the shoot, I noticed flashes of fear in her eyes. I was bubbling with excitement and inspiration from thinking about all of the creative ideas I had for the shoot, but I could sense a little bit of her hesitation, which dampened my excitement. At the time, I was left feeling confused and, in all honesty, slightly offended. Why wasn't she equally excited about her senior year photoshoot? We parted ways after our conversation, and she agreed to meet early the next morning after I explained how the lighting was best during that time of the day.

The sound of my alarm jolted me from my sleep early the next morning. I turned over, and the time glared on my home screen: 6:00 a.m.. For a brief moment, I considered ignoring the time completely and pretending that today was actually another day. As I laid there, I remembered Anna's lack of excitement in our conversation, which made the idea of falling back asleep sound that much more appealing. However, there was a bigger part of me that knew that I couldn't let her down. Slowly, begrudgingly, I forced myself out of bed and got ready for the eventful day ahead.

After triple checking to make sure my camera was fully charged, I scrambled to find my keys and left to meet Anna at an open field nearby. When I pulled into the parking lot, she was putting on the last-minute finishing touches to her makeup and outfit. As soon as she got out of the car, I was taken aback by the length of her sunset red dress that perfectly traveled up to reach her shoulders. Each fold and piece of fabric was perfectly placed, and I couldn't help but stare for a couple of seconds. She looked as close to angelic as I had ever seen.

LENS OF ADMIRATION

We started walking over to where we were going to take pictures, and I kept repeating to her how amazing she looked and how excited I was about the morning we were going to spend together. I assured her that I was going to explain exactly how I wanted her to pose to ease some of her worries. I wanted her to be as comfortable as possible in front of the camera.

I began taking pictures of her, but I could tell that she was uncomfortable. I walked her through exactly how I wanted her to position her body, but she continued to stiffen up with self-doubt. I could feel the insecurity and frustration surfacing in her. Rather than letting her walk away, I began to speak truth over her: she was beautiful. And she deserved to feel that way in this moment. I reminded her that focusing on her own beauty in this moment is something to celebrate—a chance to talk back to her mind as it tried to take her back to a place of self-doubt.

As I continued scouting out the area for the perfect location, I noticed tall, white flowers peeking over the grass from the field where we were standing. They looked like tiny daisies, ornately clothing the grass surrounding them. I jumped with joy and motioned with excitement to Anna to come and see what I had discovered. As soon as she came over, her face lit up and beamed with excitement. Almost immediately, she began to loosen up and started dancing in the grass, seemingly forgetting that I was even there. In seeing such beauty, she came alive before the camera, and her own radiance became even more palpable. Her genuine joy and comfort swept her doubts away, which completely transformed how I photographed her. Any residing insecurity or doubt I had in my own ability disappeared. We both welcomed the freedom to steadfastly, wholeheartedly love ourselves, in this very moment.

Once we finished our session, we walked back to our cars together, and I leaned over to show her some of the pictures we had created.

The images were stunning. They were some of my best work, and I was so overjoyed with how they turned out. I glanced over at Anna to see her reaction, and she lifted her glistening eyes to meet with mine.

"Grace, this is the first time I've ever felt beautiful."

I was so overwhelmed with emotion that I struggled to muster a response for her. I had found my purpose in my craft. Never in my life had something been so clearly revealed to me.

All of this time, my focus had been on the self. I imagined and chased this goal of winning prizes through my photography: the validation, the likes on Instagram, the recognition. In this moment, every reward became meaningless. My imagination paused the longing for validation and self-recognition and welcomed Anna's words to breathe life and meaning into my spirit. That feeling is one I never wanted to let go of. It was that sweet.

I realized that what I love the most about photography is how the camera allows me to portray people with sympathy. It provides me with the ability to capture both the somber and striking beauty in each person I photograph. Sometimes, simply reminding someone of their beauty isn't compelling enough. But when they see photographs of themselves instead, they see themselves in a light that is compelling. Photographs can gently invite my subjects to foster a posture of beauty, grace, and admiration in how they see themselves.

***

This entire memory flashes through my mind as I process what my friend has said about wanting the nose job. I don't think I will ever be able to convince her of her beauty through politics, compelling statistics, various research, feminist theories, or personal anecdotes.

Perhaps I can begin with a question instead.

"Can I take you to this beautiful field of grass?"

THE HARDEST PERFORMANCE

OLIVIA BLAKE

"What is your hardest performance?"

well, what even is "hard"?

is it the hardest one to portray?

the hardest "smile and wave"?

because it is all just the same

i just want to feel something

a spark

to light a fire under my butt

to shock me back to life

i'm coding

CODE BLUE!

everyone clear the patient

but i don't have the patience

to

Olivia Blake

                just

          flip

     the

switch

everything is fine

what do you need?

you're hurting?

well so am i

and so is the next guy

but this isn't about me

it is about you

so let me pack my wounds so that i may lick yours too

they say you can't pour from an empty glass

but my well has been dry for years

so i must fill it with my tears

and shift gears

onto the next objective

the next task

the next thing

just

THE HARDEST PERFORMANCE

    out

        of

            reach

because if i ever stop what will be left?

nothing?

something?

everything?

who knows and who cares

because that is a fallacy

and this is reality

where perfection isn't this far off goal

it is the expectation

one step out of line isn't fine

when everything is on the line

so,

stay with me and don't you dare flatline

i have always been told

"Close your legs"

"Sit up straight"

may not a single hair be out of place

as you should know your place

"Keep quiet", "You talk too much"

well, i am too much

"You should be seen, not heard"

but i am the black sheep of this herd

so i must continue to pull the wool over your eyes

so that i don't get prying eyes

regarding all of my white lies

"Are you okay?"

on a pain scale from 1 to 10, i want to scream i'm a 9

but instead, i respond, yes, i'm completely fine

can't you see by the smile plastered across my face that i am doing great

and not full of self-hate

because, darling, if you haven't realized yet, it is far too late

i am already gone

packed deep away

in a forgotten box in the corner of the attic of my mind

the me you know and love

hell, the me you can't stand

THE HARDEST PERFORMANCE

they are all just pawns in this game

you think we are playing checkers

but this is chess

every move is calculated

with someone else in mind

to not disturb the waters

to not rock the boat

to get in and get out

"keep your head down"

and "put your nose to the grindstone"

grind baby grind

so that others don't pay any mind

to what goes on behind closed doors

when you are utterly alone

and can't take it any more

but do not fear because when that switch is turned off and

the monsters come out to play

because they will quickly be stowed away

when the next person comes a-knocking on that door

asking you for more and more.

AFTER EDEN

MARY COSTANZA

It is the nature of all things to ripen. Time creates the sugar that makes the apple sweet and indulgent. Decay is inevitable. Left to its vices, the apple will give in to its eroding character.

Once-sweet nectar devolves into an alcoholic venom, poisoning itself and those who eat from it.

The apple is meant to be consumed, to nourish. But if left to sit, if overexposed to light and oxygen, it will play a game of deceptive revenge as its sweetness goes unacknowledged. From its soft inner-core, the apple will begin to degrade. It won't happen all at once. A few places here and there will begin to spoil. *Maybe that's okay?* It still looks like an apple. Maybe it even still feels like an apple: crisp and firm, bound and whole. Sometimes you have to be willing to take the good with the bad. If you can find a way to cut out the bad places, maybe there's still something left to enjoy?

Defenseless against its own defenses, the rotting apple will bite back with a putrid sweetness. It waits for you to come along so it can teach you a lesson in its uniquely vicious way. Slowly, the rot bleeds to the outside. We anticipate that the good will turn bad and foolishly hope we will catch it right at its sweetest point, before it's too late. Once the corruption is visible and the apple is riddled with holes, only then will we know it is irredeemable. The truth is revealed, hope is abandoned, and denial is fruitless as ripeness slides across the threshold into rot.

If you doubt what you see and grasp too tightly, your fingers will pierce through once thick skin and sink into the mush. Exploring with your fingers inside the rottenness, you'll find dark black seeds whose hard outer-shell protects them from the spoiling bacteria they swim in. What happens if you plant them? Perhaps a tree will grow nourished by the sun, water, and healthy soil. If you wait long enough and hold on to hope, you may find yourself with a sweet, freshly picked apple that's ready to nourish you.

What is the half-life of perfection? How long does it take for something good and sweet and nourishing to steadily decay into a fraction of what it once was? What is left in its absence? *Can nothing ever be enough?*

***

"Are you a dancer?"

I'm never fully comfortable answering this question. "Yes" is both too limiting and an over-exaggeration I feel I have not earned. The few moments when I have chosen to answer "yes" and honestly meant it were accompanied by an overwhelming sense of pride. But the feeling never lasts as shame slides in to take its place.

"No," however, feels like a betrayal of all the hours, effort, heartache, and joy I have poured into my craft. Saying "no" is an act of protest, but I'm not sure who it is I'm fighting. Myself or the questioner? My experiences or another's assumptions? "No" has become my defense against the all-consuming nature of the identity, or what I presumed was my identity.

Neither answer is satisfying. Their partial truth leaves me wanting for more and feeling as though I've made a promise I'm bound to break. *Do I owe my whole self to my passion?*

AFTER EDEN

Ballet presents an unending tension between the resentment I feel towards my identity as a dancer and my desire not to lose the nourishing sense of awe and wonder I experience in the art form. As an essential part of my faith, ballet makes me feel whole. I find comfort in the certainty of its rituals the same way others do with their religion. The studio is my temple. Plies are my prayers, offered daily. Passed down as a fragile oral tradition, the classical canon is my sacred scripture, telling the story of who I should be and what is possible. In this faith, there is no room for doubt. After all, I traded Jesus Christ for George Balanchine. For Balanchine, when we make the choice to dance, our souls are at stake. He swears "la danse, madame, c'est une question morale." Our inadequacy carries the shame of sin and demands repentance. When we fail to achieve salvation in the studio and on the stage, we repent our disgraceful lack of fortitude and lapse in devotion. We are to blame for our own damnation.

When you pursue excellence in ballet, the art form is no longer something you do. Rather, the discipline dictates who you become—excellence demands devotion and sacrifice. This identity is constructed for you by dancers across generations, so I embraced all of the trappings of what I thought it meant to be an artist in this lifetime without fully knowing what it entailed. Once I decided that a dancer was who I wanted to be, every other decision seemed to be made for me.

As a young dancer, my only job was to learn how to imitate the steps I saw my instructors make. Through the looking glass, I reflected back to them their youth and talent. Without question, I walked the path of those who came before me and trusted it would get me where I wanted to be. Every action—both within the studio and without—was endowed with sacred significance and a sense of certainty that promised to bring me closer to the perfect ideal. *Who decided the ideal? Just another dancer with a god-complex.*

Dancers have to love what they do and find fulfillment in the work because, with the demands made by ballet, that's all they have. As Merce Cunningham reminds us, "you have to love dancing to stick to it. It gives you nothing back, no manuscripts to store away, no paintings to show on walls and maybe hang in museums, no poems to be printed and sold, nothing but that single fleeting moment when you feel alive." Our world of meaning is limited to the dancing reflections hanging from the stained-glass walls of floor to ceiling mirrors, images that are often distorted by the streaks and smudges of the other dancers' sweaty bodies. Exploring other aspects of myself signaled an impoverished innerlife. *What more could I possibly want?* Intensified by the constant partnership of our own reflection, no mistake or insecurity can be avoided. Like Narcissus with his devastatingly beautiful image, we forget that the art form isn't capable of loving us in return. At least not in the way we love it. True love redeems us, but this is a judgmental love, a conditional love, a suffocating love. So, I waited at the threshold of passion and obsession because love told me everything was at stake.

I learned as a little girl that beauty was the ultimate aim. There is no beauty without sacrifice.

The art form made its demands, and there was nothing I wouldn't do to appease it. Most of the time, both ballet and myself felt impossible to please. So I gave and I gave until I felt I had nothing left to give. I felt like I had to earn the honor of being a dancer, so no amount of work was too great. I didn't think about everything I was choosing to sacrifice in order to make the incremental progress that was getting me closer to perfection. I didn't allow myself to believe it mattered. Nothing else could possibly matter as much as who I was on the stage. I viewed myself and my own narrow perfectibility through an artistic lens that blinded me to everything else.

AFTER EDEN

Unable to recognize beauty outside of myself, this tenet became my own twisted justification.

The Voice of the tradition crept into the soft inner-workings of my mind until all that existed was a clearly defined inner Voice urging me into the person I needed to be to pursue perfection. In its grip, every other thought turned to mush. It could be my fiercest champion or my harshest critic as it sharpened my focus and demanded my sacrifices. It spread through my consciousness and touched everything that I was. A depression marks the places of pressure. After some time, there was no competition between this seemingly divine Voice and my own. I willingly welcomed it in. Solemnly bowed in its presence, I waited for it to speak to me, offer its consolation, and acknowledge my piety. In response, the Voice boomed that I was never talented enough, never turned out enough, never thin enough, never good enough, never enough.

From pliés to grand jetés, young dancers are reminded of the great distance that lies between where we are and where we are working to be. That realization is both the agony and the ecstasy of the process. "Prove you aren't expendable. Work harder!" When it comes to the pursuit of perfection, casual effort just won't do the job! The physical challenges we face are not nearly as daunting as the mental games we have to play with ourselves to keep going. Amidst the ache of injury, physical and emotional exhaustion, I told my crying body, "It doesn't hurt that bad. Just shake it off and run the variation again. *What kind of artist am I if I can't romanticize the pain?*" Gelsey Kirkland, that graceless saint of the ballet world, did.

Because ballet is so inextricably linked to who we are, dancers learn to justify the sacrifices to prove our piety in the hope that we can remain cloistered away with our sacred community for a while longer. The practice is constructed in such a way that dancers are kept submissive and childlike. No ballet master has all the answers, but because dancers are forbidden to ask questions, the instructor's ignorance is unimportant and remains unchallenged. *I certainly wasn't brave enough to test wits with god.* It's a cruel form of gatekeeping where the sacrificial victim tends to be your own identity and sense of self. *Who are we if not dancers?*

Made in their divine image, the dancers who came before us defined what it meant to be fully human. Our passion to be more than human informed every decision we made. When it came to choosing between our humanity and our artistry, the answer seemed obvious. The daily ritual of ballet technique class is a transcendent experience. You are wholly present in your body as it breathes through the motions of the repertoire while at the same time you feel detached from your physical being. No longer your own, your body becomes a tool for telling someone else's story. Observing yourself in the mirror and ruminating in your own head, you become an omniscient third-party making endless observations and critiques. You are limitless as the energy extends long past the ends of your fingertips and down through the line of your pointe shoes. Not even gravity can pin you to the earth. In this lifetime, it's the closest we come to encountering the divine. Dancers are playing God as we engage in our own sacred form of world-making. This ritual is demanding, but it serves as a testament to our belief that perfection is a possibility instead of some abstract ideal. We aim for perfect practice in hopes of carving ourselves into the exalted image of a ballet dancer. Only once perfection is realized will you feel like you deserve to be "a dancer." Only then can we achieve eschaton, the revelation of perfection manifest.

In order to keep choosing the art form, I came to see the process as a necessary evil that would get me where I wanted to be. I would do anything. I was willing to trust anyone that said they could make me the dancer I desperately wanted to be.

I would trust anyone. Even a snake.

When a snake enters the garden in which you were planted, in which you were cultivated, in which you ripened, you don't always recognize the venom at once. Whether the venom is addiction, manipulation, or violence, it's not always possible to protect yourself, or even recognize that protection is needed and deserved. Perhaps it was my youth, my desire to prove how dedicated I was to my art, or my trust that the people in my life loved me and cared enough to know what was best for me—even better than I knew myself—that led me to accept the cruelty I received and justify it as an attempt to toughen my mind and make me a better dancer.

Desperation blurred the lines between malice and tough love.

The response that this mistreatment begged from me was an obsession with trying to do more and push myself further to prove that I was as dedicated as I thought I needed to be to merit being treated any differently, to be treated with kindness and respect, to be treated like "a dancer." I was truly rotten with perfection.

The harder I worked, the worse the abuse got and the more saccharin I became. In retrospect, the cruelty was never about ballet, but because ballet was every ounce of my life and who I was, I thought it had everything to do with the art form and my place in it. I clung to my belief in this perverted sense of justice. If I was going through hell, it's because hell is exactly what I deserved. I blamed myself for my broken heart. I still blame myself for the time and love lost, but unlike Giselle, I refuse to allow heartache to disrupt my peace of mind. Ballet passed its judgements, and I conceded because it was the only metric I had. I accepted this false narrative as Gospel truth. Blindly dependent on its worldview, I had no choice but to trust its standards and modes of critique however irrational they seemed. "You're not having a good day. Don't look at yourself in the mirror," I would tell myself, blaming my confusion and restless unease on some meaningless physical imperfection and waging war against my body as a result. *Forgive me, for I did not know what I was doing.* Because ballet was the only world I knew and I was desperate to see myself achieve salvation within it, my solutions didn't aim at changing my world and getting out of the toxic garden in which I was growing, ripening, and turning to rot. In my mind, I could tolerate whatever bad came my way as long as I still had my dancing—as long as I was still in the garden.

Justifying the unbearable with false hope, I tried to carve out spaces that I thought the rot couldn't touch. I began to travel during the summer to receive the training I desired but was missing during the traditional school year. "Just make it through the year, and it will all be okay this summer," I convinced myself. The new experiences I created took me to the most otherworldly places—the gilded studios of American Ballet Theatre's 890 Broadway and backstage at Lincoln Center where I watched Apollo's angels prepare for flight—and gave me the opportunity to explore my love for ballet under the influence of some of the most exemplary ballet legends: Julie Kent, Franco DeVita, Robert Barnett. These artists served as embodied examples that both the joy and heartache were worth something greater. I would have sold my soul to train and dance like them with their spider-thin limbs, effortlessly bent into willowing lines that branched out from their elegant bodies. They shined as they piquéd en arabesque and smoothed the transition into multiple pirouettes. The ease with which they appeared to move was a testament to their hard work, refined technique, and lifetime of secrets. Dancers are the ultimate performers. In our lives and in our art, there is no such thing as an honest performance. To expose the truth would be to distort the magic. I was taught to put on a brave face, to be seen and never heard. This is the fraud that allows me to take the seemingly impossible and make it look easy, beautiful even. Even on my bad days, my audiences are none the wiser.

While on pilgrimage, I experienced different training styles, techniques, and new repertoires in environments where the mutual passion for our craft filled every studio. The days were long and grueling, but my efforts finally felt worth it, as I had a space and time away from the toxicity of my home studio. These truly sacred spaces served as a second chance where I could continue to develop my own talent and renew my love for ballet in a place where I felt at home in my practice and my body.

Summer after summer, I stepped out of my normal life and routine. I would return to communities where my own dedication was acknowledged and shared by the other dancers in the room. As fundamentalists, we clung to our unerring truths for their sense of artistry and wonder. As bastions of the tradition, we felt a deep, aching need to force these truths onto others. We shared the understanding that ballet was perfection in progress. But still, progress never seemed good enough. No longer were we content to only encounter the Divine. Impatiently, we were working to become gods. Desperately, we labored to shape ourselves into the false idols that inhabited the stages of our dreams.

The feeling of being connected with the other dancers as we attempted to shape our minds and bodies to endure the long days of rehearsal and the tireless pursuit of bettering ourselves was something I lacked at my home studio. When I would return to my studio for the school year, I was treated like a pariah because I was completely dedicated to ballet and saw it as an end in itself—it was my religion and I was the zealot. Friendship was nearly impossible.

The pressures of competition often turn dancer against dancer. Everyone watched with anticipation as they hoped to see me fail and lose my religion. Those for whom watching and waiting wasn't enough decided to pick up sticks and poke at me to see what it would take to finally get me to bite. Surely, they seemed to think, humiliation or bodily harm would do it. Once I was back in the garden and knew the truth about its borders, night fell and I entered a long period of loneliness and deep social isolation. Once you've been banished, you can't go home again.

While I had originally become rotten with perfection and in constant pursuit, when I began to reach my goals I was met with pain, resistance, and isolation. *No matter what I do, it'll never be good enough.* I became rotten with imperfection, and I no longer saw any meaning in my efforts. Any value was shrouded in the mistreatment I was facing. I still loved the art form, but I began to feel as though there was no place for me in it. I didn't want to quit, but I also didn't know if I could continue. It was my own confused crisis of faith. The garden tried to take what I loved more than anything in the world from me. This interruption to my identity left me feeling incomplete and aimless. Things went silent. My life as a dancer was no longer about the joy that I found in the art form. Rather, the work became a constant battle of trying to prove myself. I'd lost sight of what was originally meaningful and compelling about the art form. This lapse in faith carved out a deep hole. Where there once was love and devotion, apathy and fear slid in to take their place. I was rotten to the core.

I was absorbed in the awe of classical ballet. Without words ballet is able to tell a story, take you out of this world, and create a more perfect one. For me, that dream is what made my time spent rotting in the garden worth it. It was the sense of hope that promised I could enjoy those fleeting moments of perfection—that perfection was even possible this side of eternity. Hope is the foundation of my belief in perfection. Without hope, no dancer would be able to meet the art form's demands and tirelessly work to create and re-create themselves. In a bleeding world, an artist's hope calls us to make a choice to be more, to be better, to be complete, to believe in the potential of our perfection, and to nurture one another's perfectibility. However, we must not allow ourselves to become rotten with it.

I had been too busy listening to the Voice in my head. I failed to realize there would come a time when the grand curtain would fall for my final performance, I would take my final reverence, and it would be up to me to figure out who I was going to be. I didn't want to be standing up on a dark stage with the curtain closed—clueless, aimless, and banished. An exile.

If I wanted any chance of knowing who that girl would be, I needed to silence the inner Voice and replace it with something new. In the silence, I listened and quietly heard new voices begin to whisper to me through the healing rhythms of philosophy, literature, and poetry.

"Tenderness and rot share a border..." poet Kay Ryan's voice rings in my ear.

"It is important to stay sweet and loving." She reminds me in her poetic truth.

Voltaire chimes in:

"One must cultivate one's own garden,"

Satirizing the naive optimism I once knew so well.

Gwendolyn Brooks joins the chorus, reflecting on performer-turned-activist in "Paul Robeson."

"We are each other's harvest:" she says.

"We are each other's business:" she instructs.

"We are each other's magnitude and bond." My only option was to uproot.

I should have left sooner, but it was the evil I knew and there was a strange comfort in that. Every day, I knew what demons lurked and how to confront the uncertainty and challenges presented. "What if you leave and never find anywhere else to dance?" "Who are you if not a dancer?" and "How will you ever be good enough for anything else?" were ever-present fears that leached off of my own insecurities. The questions implied cruel, unsatisfying answers. But finally after too many years, it became too difficult to make the choice to continue to show up every day. I feared that if I stayed in this liminal space of coming and going any longer I would end up hating ballet and march myself past the point of ruin. I didn't know who would be left in its absence. Ballet is at the center of my universe. The arts are how I make sense of my soul. When I finally left, I had to regain the ability to be my own judge and figure out who I was. I needed to take Gelsey Kirkland's advice: "study something other than ballet, and use your mind. Try to become an artist and not just a dancer. You won't find the answers in the steps themselves." I needed to develop my own voice and not allow it to genuflect before others.

I now choose to unearth the parts of myself I have given up in my efforts to prove myself. I know that if I am going to learn what it means to be fully human, I need to live completely. Having ballet as the only aspect of my humanity isn't going to create true wholeness. It is simply offering me an illusion.

Since the beginning of the Covid pandemic, distance from the art form has given rise to feelings of homelessness and spiritual dislocation, but the space has also provided a new perspective and sense of clarity that isn't available when I am looking from up close. In spite of my nostalgia, I now see that distance is what I needed to arrive at the truth. My false hope was the price I had to pay for truth, and my truth bears the weight of its own heavy cross. This parting has shown me that having my identity wrapped up in one thing for so long was as punishing and limiting as it was fulfilling and meaningful. I now see that it is no longer worth it to find an answer to the question "Are you a dancer?" if being "a dancer" is the only identity that matters to me.

Abandoning my reliance on absolutes, I have begun to care more and more about my own nuance. I am learning to answer "yes, and" or the occasional "no, but" when asked to define myself, and I see how much more meaning I can create in a well-integrated life. While I work to fit the pieces of my life back together, I'm learning to embrace my honest imperfections as the promise of my redeemability instead of that which is damning me and worth hiding in shame. What's more, I realize that if I continue to allow perfection to be defined by the boundaries of a spoiled garden, more important aspects of my character will be pruned away.

Through my wandering, I stumbled my way into new gardens with fertile soil where I came to trust that I would be able to grow and flourish. Once I replanted in spaces where I was able to be kind to myself, honor beauty outside of myself, love and be loved in return, the more I was able to develop as a human being alongside my growth as an artist. I began to explore other passions with the same intensity and dedication that ballet had ingrained in me. I took my love of the arts, creativity, and deep engagement, and I developed spaces to honor those values within my academic pursuits. My love of classical music pushed me to explore the music that supports the dance, and I began to play the piano. In an attempt to heal my relationship with ballet and myself, I became a mentor to a group of young ballerinas, and I guided them through their dance training in a way that developed a love of the art form despite its demands. I felt as though I had a responsibility to communicate the lessons I learned the hard way to keep my girls from repeating my mistakes. I tried to help them see that the daily practice of cultivating the kind of person they want to step out into the world as is every bit as artistic as crafting who they are when they grace the stage. No longer a monastic, the world is now my studio and my stage; every moment is practice for my next performance. A good, honest performance will require nothing less than being fully human. My arts training has always been life training.

More important than the experiences I had and the skills I have acquired, I have stopped underestimating my ability to wrestle with discomfort and uncertainty. The more I have thrown myself into following other pursuits, the more confident I have become with my solitude. I now know that my worth isn't dependent on my performance in the dance studio or how well I meet other people's expectations for me. I am beginning to recognize my worth based on the totality of who I am instead of solely basing it on one small part of myself, as I am tending a life that is vast enough to hold the complexity and contradiction of every joy and sorrow. While I still find myself chasing perfection, I realize that it won't be achieved in any wholehearted way if I only care about finding it in one domain. Letting myself venture out of the garden to explore has been an act of reclaiming my soul–a soul I am replanting in the hope that it will sprout and, in a process of becoming, grow into something sweet that nourishes myself and those around me. In the absence of perfection, my soul is what I have left. I'll confess that at times I still feel a bit bruised, but at my core I hold on to the belief that this seed might be enough.

Everyone finds themselves originally planted in a garden. We

AFTER EDEN

accept the sacred and the profane because that is what we know. It informs so much of who we are becoming, and oftentimes we believe that making the choice between staying and leaving is an act of sacrilege. It's difficult to live the questions when the act of questioning feels like heresy. We have faith that the garden will nourish us and provide for our flourishing, but sometimes we find ourselves planted in an unholy Eden where snakes slither about and once-sweet fruit lays on the ground putrefying under the glare of a hot sun. If we allow this garden to unquestioningly make its demands based on the certainty of our faith, this bounded awareness of perfection becomes a broken promise because true flourishing is never a possibility here. We owe it to ourselves and to those around us to flourish. We deserve to flourish. So our faith must allow room for doubt because sometimes the best choice we can make is to imagine the possibility of a new garden, uproot, and replant. We must cultivate our own gardens. We are each other's harvest. Stay sweet and loving.

SO THE STONES CRY OUT

ANN PHELPS

Sunday morning. I hurry a few paces ahead, with each crunching step drawing me closer to the clearing that is just around the corner. The childish chatter blends back into the trees behind me, and I breathe deeper, knowing their dad can handily manage both of them alone, certainly for a few minutes, even on top of a mountain. Just a few rare and sacred moments of solitude as I emerge to behold the layered horizon of grey-blue ridges before me, fading out into the hazy distance.

I pause and pull the cool air into my lungs. I try to focus on my breathing. I strive to exhale fully, situating myself in the present. I work my very hardest to ground myself, mindful of the mountain holding me up, solid under my feet. I try and try and try to stop thinking. I work to stop trying. I strive to stop working. Contemplate! Reflect! Now! Before your kids round the corner and demand you shout and sing and yodel like Maria Von Trap into the cavern below so we can hear our echoes! Be in the now! Be present! Just do it!

It isn't working. But if anyone can engage in immediate and instantaneous contemplation, it should be me!

I have spent too many Sunday mornings rehearsing this hurried pace, as I rushed around looking for some choir member's lost folder, or giving feedback to a piano tuner attempting to *un-tune* a piano in order to match to an old organ's waning pitch, or listening back from the center of a huge sanctuary as a jazz quintet attempts to adapt its reedy, rhythmic resonance to the demands of a soaring stone space built for still small voices of boys choirs and low drones of well-articulated sermons. None of these mornings were full of mindfulness or contemplation for me, despite the fact that when the church bells chimed—whether sounding throughout some rolling English countryside or tolling from a spire and bouncing around the skyscrapers of downtown Manhattan—my job was to instantly calm at the ringing of those bells. I was the liturgist, the soloist, the cantor. My call was to create not the illusion, but the *reality* of mindful, sacred worship for all who walked through the doors, whether pilgrims or regulars or confused tourists. Center yourself quickly so others can gather. I was well rehearsed in having ten-to-thirty seconds to transform from a bustling staff member to a calm, steady voice of invocation of the divine.

But this Sunday, I was not in the nave. I was hiking with my family. My days of thick robes and handbells were over. Or at least on hold, as in-person worship and any communal singing had been banned. Another casualty of the Covid season or, as the high-church, liturgical calendar-following folks like to call it: Coronatide.

Those who know me well have, over the years, inquired as to how I found myself in such an unusual occupation, particularly those who observed my propensity to duck out of the Saturday night scene early, despite my extroversion and the joy I find in socializing and community, in order to be able to be up before dawn to attend a church in a tradition I don't even claim as my own. They wonder, "How did you become . . . a church musician and service coordinator? A liturgical jazz singer? An interfaith cantor? A gospel improviser? (And more recently) a virtual voice in a recorded Zoom box?"

My typical response has been, "Well, churches pay better than bars," a cheeky aside to distract from the complicated undercurrents that have drawn me in and out the doors of churches over the years. It gets a laugh, and gets at some kernel of truth, as most jokes do. I did first enter the job market during the Great Recession, and the only thing folks would reliably pay me to do for a few years was sing. And my avoidance of the question wasn't an attempt to skirt inquiries about my faith or doubts or grappling with organized religion—that's a conversation I'll have with anyone. If you don't believe me, set aside several hours and give me a call. The dodging is due to the fact that I'm not always sure why I've done this with my time and energy, with my life. It has taken me to beautiful, sacred spaces all over the world and quiet unknown corners of the spiritual lives of strangers. I wouldn't trade it, and the sacrifices have been minor if anything at all. But how one finds themselves in these spaces in the first place is more difficult to fathom.

As a cantor, my task is not to perform for audiences who are rapt or moved or even inspired by my voice. I am here to sing in a way that invites others to join me. I am to create a space for other voices to fill, leading them with a confidence that puts them at ease, and as they enter the song, my job is to get lost in the tides of singing. To make myself heard in order to become as quickly inaudible. To be seen with the goal of becoming invisible. It is an extrovert's dream to put themselves out there not to be judged but to be joined, as we come together to do something so much larger than ourselves.

The truth is, I struggle to know who I am in isolation. I don't want to be alone on a stage with a single spotlight. I certainly don't want to lock myself in my home, away from a community so that I can adhere to the necessary but soul-sucking protocols so aptly and depressingly named "social distancing." I don't even know what I think until I call my mom or text my sisters or ramble at my spouse to find clarity. In order to know my ideas, I need to articulate them to someone else and hear them echoed back to me in love. And the same is true for what I feel. When I am alone, feelings, internal sensations of some kind, rush around my consciousness and through my body like trapped animals. But when I gather my breath and release a melody into the world, they are set free. And when others join me in that refrain, my intangible feelings become real tangible waves of sound moving the air and reverberating through bodies. Regardless of the words we are singing, the sound we are making becomes my emotional experience of the world, and I know who I am.

Another liturgist and theologian I like a lot, Don Saliers, talks about how what we believe lives somewhere between or around what we think *and* what we feel. Ours is a culture that has somehow reduced religion to the assertion of beliefs, often neglecting the role that tradition, ritual, community, practice, and so many other elements play in religious spaces. Simultaneously, we have created a secular world that makes it nearly impossible to believe anything as we question everything we know, including who has the truth and whether they are telling it. Whether it is healthy critical thinking or the assertion of alternative facts, we can never be sure what to be sure of. We don't know what we believe because we don't know what to think and we don't know how we feel.

Other liturgical types I've spent time with over the years respond by going back to the Latin: *lex orandi, lex credendi*. As we pray, so we believe. The idea is that the prayers we utter together, in community, become what we believe, even if only by habit and repetition. But if Don is onto something, the prayers we sing and set to emotional music, become the stuff of real belief, dancing in that space between and around our thoughts and our feelings.

There were many mornings I walked into a church, coffee in hand, eyes still a bit bleary from sleep, completely unsure of what I believed. But I would stand and sing: *benedictus qui venit, in nomine domine*... Blessed is the one who comes in the name of the Lord... I didn't really know what else I believed, but I would hear the stone rafters of the cathedral sing back to me, with their nearly eight seconds of reverb. I still rarely completely know what I believe, but years of Sundays here have taught me that these were the words the crowds shouted to Jesus when he entered Jerusalem, provoking the authorities to command him to shut his people up before they started a riot. But he retorts, "If these people were silent, even the stones would cry out."

On those Sundays, I could hear my voice ring back from the stone pillars: *Hosanna in excelsis!* Hosanna in the highest. The word Hosanna is nonsense, really, to someone like me. An ambiguous term of adoration, rooted in ancient Hebrew, with no exact translation in any language I actually know. Again: I don't always know what I believe. But if I draw in the breath and release it back into the world as song, I hear the whole earth and the crowds around me cry out in adoration and praise for what *is*. In this moment. Hosanna in excelsis, indeed. I might not know what I think and cannot name what I feel, but in this moment I believe in this act of hope.

And in this nonsensical, unknown and unknowable place, gratitude abounds.

As I exhale, I hear the small footsteps of my two kids breaking my reverie, catching up with me, bringing me back from the cathedral to the mountaintop. "Mom! Mommyyyyyyyyy!" they cry, and their small, high voices bounce back from the ridges of mountains beyond.

I realize I did it. I reflected. I centered. And now I am here, in the present. Now my job is to make space for them to do the same. It is Sunday morning again, and I am the cantor.

They join me in the clearing, and with no choir folders to locate or instruments to tune, we embark in our new tradition at the top of the mountain. We sing our silly nonsense into the void and hear the stones cry back. And with everything I am—my voice, my breath, my bones and even my brain—I believe in all of it.

Acknowledgments

We want to thank the many collaborators and contributors to this volume that was slow and steady in the making during a pandemic that has been slow and steady in progression. We are grateful to Adarian, Brianna, Grace, Leanna, Liat, Olivia, Sarah, and Whitney who wrote beautiful submissions and stuck with the project through writing circles, editing sessions, and delay after delay that we all became accustomed to in a Covid-riddled world. I, Ann, want to especially thank two contributors: Katherine, whose original idea grew into this beautiful community and whose leadership turned an impulse into a sustained experience, and Mary, who started this as a student and concluded it as a staff member and editor who took on tremendous logistical and emotional labor that somehow resulted in a beautiful and seemingly effortless creative performance. These two dancers have clearly been well trained in ways that will carry through all their endeavors. We also want to thank Hannah Lafferrandre for her creative, logistical, and personal support in the earliest days of the Covid shutdown.

We are grateful to Library Partners Press for their enthusiastic partnership, Felix Mooneeram for the striking cover photo, and the John Templeton Foundation and Lilly Endowment, Inc. for their financial support of the Program for Leadership and Character generally, and our work in character and the arts specifically. The opinions expressed in this publication are those of the authors and do not necessarily reflect the views of the John Templeton Foundation, Lilly Endowment, Inc., or Wake Forest University.

We also want to thank the Wake the Arts movement, our incredible team at the Program for Leadership and Character for making this work so meaningful and enjoyable, the Wake Forest administrators, faculty and staff who have inspired and mentored these students and in performance and writing and whose impact pervades these pages, and supporters of the Program for Leadership and Character whose partnership has made this creative work possible. We are grateful to be at a university that makes both character and the arts central to what it means to be "for humanity."

Finally, we thank Christina Soriano and Michael Lamb for their writing, editing, and administrative support and encouragement, and April Stace for her love of words and people that allows them both to come to life on the page. Her vulnerable example, care for students, and creative brilliance have shaped every part of this project, and her ongoing friendship has tremendous impacts beyond this project. We are beyond thankful for all these contributors whose empathy, authenticity, honesty, humor, and brilliance lent meaning to an otherwise confounding year and illuminated the beauty and goodness in the world. Now as much as ever: gratitude abounds.